1. A pair of Tornado GR.1s of No. 9 Squadron RAF en route for bombing practice over the West Freugh range in 1983. The aircraft are carrying 1,000lb retarded bombs under the fuselage, long-range tanks on the inner pylons and a pair of Sky Shadow ECM pods on the outer pylons. A BOZ decoy dispenser pod would replace the starboard ECM pod as stocks became available. (BAe)

WARBIRDS ILLUSTRATED No 42

Tornado

MICHAEL J. GETHING

ARMS AND ARMOUR PRESS

Introduction

First published in Great Britain in 1987 by Arms and Armour Press Ltd., Link House, West Street, Poole, Dorset BH15 1LL.

Distributed in the USA by Sterling Publishing Co. Inc., 2 Park Avenue, New York, NY 10016.

Distributed in Australia by Capricorn Link (Australia) Pty. Ltd., P.O. Box 665, Lane Cove, New South Wales 2066.

British Library Cataloguing in Publication data:
Gething, Michael J.
Tornado.—(Warbirds illustrated; 42)
1. Tornado (Jet fighter plane)—History
I. Title   II. Series
623.74'64   UG1242.F5

ISBN 0-85368-788-9

Edited and designed by Roger Chesneau; typeset by Typesetters (Birmingham) Ltd.; printed and bound in Italy in association with Keats European Production Ltd., London.

◀2
2. A study in variable geometry: two RAF and one Luftwaffe Panavia Tornado IDS aircraft from the Tri-national Tornado Training Establishment (TTTE) based at RAF Cottesmore swing their wings for the camera, January 1981. (Sgt. Brian Lawrence)

The Tornado is remarkable in many ways. It is a true multi-role combat aircraft, and was known as MRCA for several years before being christened Tornado in March 1976. It was born out of a vital need for rationalization of equipment within NATO and is, indeed, international. The manufacturers, Panavia GmbH, are a consortium of British Aerospace (BAe), Messerschmitt-Bölkow-Blohm (MBB) and Aeritalia (AIT), while the engines are built by Turbo-Union, formed by Rolls-Royce, Motoren und Turbinen Union (MTU) and Fiat. Apart from the final assembly lines for complete aircraft, there is no duplication of manufacture within the programme.

Tornado has proved that collaboration *can* work to produce a combat aircraft to satisfy the needs of four air arms. To do this, two basic designs were evolved, the interdictor-strike (IDS) aircraft and the air defence variant (ADV). In addition to the nine prototypes and six pre-series aircraft, 805 production aircraft were initially required. Four of the pre-series aircraft are to be refurbished and bought up to full production standard, and the resulting 809 aircraft are being distributed as follows: 96 IDS for the German *Marineflieger* and 228 IDS for the *Luftwaffe*; 100 IDS for the *Aeronautica Militare Italiana*; and 220 IDS (GR.1) and 165 ADV (18 F.2/2A plus 147 F.3) for the RAF.

Despite several attempts to sell Tornado to Canada, Australia, Spain and Greece, the first export order (for the RAF's ADV) came from Oman in August 1985, with a modest eight and an option on another eight. A month later in September, Saudi Arabia signed a Memorandum of Understanding with the UK to supply a 'package deal' of aircraft consisting of 48 Tornado IDS, 24 ADVs, 30 Hawk trainers and 30 PC-9 trainers. As we close for press, it is quite probable that Jordan will sign for a mix of both types, having had a request for US equipment rejected. Panavia is also leading a bid for 40 aircraft for Turkey, while Japan is looking at Tornado as well. It has also been announced that Germany is beginning the development of a third major type, the Electronic Combat/Reconnaissance (ECR) variant, for which there is now an order for 35 aircraft. Air arms are at last becoming aware that Tornado is an aircraft worth having.

Indeed, the most recent testimonials to the Tornado are the results achieved by the RAF in the 1984 and 1985 USAF Strategic Air Command annual bombing competitions. In the three events for which the aircraft was eligible, the RAF on both occasions came first in two and second in the other. As might be expected, many of Tornado's critics came from the United States, and this successful performance has proved that the Tornado cannot be dismissed out of hand.

I have been fortunate to have followed the Tornado's progress since 1973, having witnessed certain 'milestones' in person and spoken with many people involved in the programme over that time. This book presents a photographic record of the aircraft's development and service record to date. I wish to acknowledge, with grateful thanks, the assistance of the following, either specifically for this book or generally since 1973: Folkhard Oelwein of Panavia; Wolfram Wolf of MBB; Alfredo Mingione of Aeritalia; Alex Johnston (now retired), Geoffrey Hill and David Kamiya of British Aerospace; Barry Ellson of RAF Germany; HQ, RAF Strike Command; Richard L. Ward of Modeldecal; and Pete Cooper and David Mason of BARG.

Once upon a time I heard MRCA being spelt out as 'Mother Riley's Cardboard Aeroplane'. No longer is the Tornado so scorned. It has proved itself in service, and long may it remain in service.

Michael J. Gething

▲ 3   ▼ 4

3. A very early artist's impression of the Multi-Role Combat Aircraft (MRCA) being developed by Panavia from 1969. (Panavia)

4. An early 1970s model of the MRCA (then designated Panavia 200) posed over a photograph of Salmesbury airfield, a satellite of Warton, where the BAC (later BAe) component of Panavia is located. The wings are in the fully forward, landing position. (BAe)

5. The first officially released photograph of the MRCA appeared in late April 1974. The prototype P-01, D-9591, is seen here at MBB's Manching flight test centre in Germany. (Panavia)

6. Another view of P-01 at Manching, released at the Hanover Air Show in May 1974. Configured as an interdictor-strike (IDS) aircraft, the shape remains virtually unchanged in 1986. (MBB)

5▲ 6▼

▲7   ▼8

7. P-01 takes to the air for its maiden flight on 14 August 1974 with BAC project test pilot Paul Millett at the controls and MBB's Nils Meister in the second seat. The 30-minute flight from Manching in southern Germany was trouble-free. Paul Millett said afterwards 'The aircraft handled superbly well – there were no problems'. (Panavia)

8. The first prototype MRCA (as it was then still called) on its maiden flight from MBB's flight test centre at Manching in Germany. (Panavia)

9. A view of P-01 at Manching on the occasion of the first press facility to see the aircraft on 21 September 1974. (Tim Wrixon)

10. A view of P-01, in *Luftwaffe* camouflage and with the German military serial 98+04, surrounded by some of the offensive weaponry it can carry, at the Paris Air Show in 1983. (Author)

11. The second prototype, P-02 (XX946), was assembled at Warton and is seen here on its first flight on 30 October 1974 with its wings fully swept. Paul Millett was again at the controls, but he was accompanied by Pietro Trevisan, Aeritalia's project pilot. Earlier that month, British Prime Minister Harold Wilson called the MRCA 'one of the wonder birds of aviation, and that's agreed to not only by us, but our partners abroad'. (BAe)

9 ▲

10 ▲ 11 ▼

▲12

12. With undercarriage gear extended, P-02 takes off for a development flight. Note the leading- and trailing-edge slats and flaps, together with the intake side doors. An afterburner cone from one of the RB.199 turbofan engines is just discernible. (BAe)

13. This fine study of P-02 during a test flight shows the wings fully swept and the large fin to advantage. (BAe)

14. Once initial flight tests were completed, P-02 began to be seen carrying the underwing stores it would use operationally. In this photograph two 330-gallon (1,500l) drop tanks are visible under the wings and four low-drag 1,000lb (453kg) bombs can be seen on the two tandem underfuselage pylons. (BAe)

▼15   ▲16

15. A pair of prototypes: P-02 and P-03 (in camouflage) side by side at Warton in 1975. P-03 (RAF serial XX947) was also the first MRCA to feature dual controls. (BAe)

16. P-03 was the first of four prototype MRCAs to fly during 1975. It made its first flight from Warton on 5 August that year with David Eagles, BAC's MRCA Project Pilot, at the controls, and with Tim Ferguson, Deputy Chief Test Pilot, in the second seat. The aircraft is seen here landing at the end of the 66-minute flight. Note the tri-national roundel carried on the nose of the aircraft. (BAe)

17. This air-to-air photograph of P-03 during its first flight emphasizes the large fin on the MRCA. The aircraft was used for assessing handling and stability, monitoring engine development and progressively expanding the flight envelope, as well as for evaluating the conversion training role. (BAe)

▲18 ▼19

20▲

18. The first prototype to feature the integrated advanced avionics suite (including the Texas Instruments terrain-following radar) was P-04, which first took to the air on 2 September 1975. This aircraft was the second German prototype, D-9592, and was flown by MBB's Chief Test Pilot, Hans-Friedrich Rammensee, with Nils Meister in the second seat. (BAe)

19. A ground view of P-04 showing the aircraft being moved to its static display location at the 1976 Hanover Air Show. Note the masking drapes over the cockpit console. (Author)

20. As P-04 continued into the development programme, it was repainted in German Navy (*Marineflieger*) colours, was re-serialled 98+05, and embarked on the integration of the AS-34 Kormoran anti-ship missile system. Four Kormorans, as illustrated here, are the principle weapons for *Marineflieger* Tornados. (MBB)

21. Italy entered the flight test programme on 5 December 1975 when the first MRCA assembled by Aeritalia – P-05 – flew from Caselle in northern Italy. Pietro Trevisan made the flight solo, accompanied by test gear in the second cockpit. (AIT)

21▼

 ▲ 22   ▼ 23

22. Like other aircraft in the programme, P-05 was to later adopt a camouflage scheme. This was applied after a rebuild which followed what Panavia described as a 'heavy landing' (but could more accurately be termed a crash) in January 1976 which fortunately occurred at Caselle. In March 1978 P-05 was returned to the flight test programme. (AIT)

23. The third British-assembled prototype, P-06 (XX948), flew from Warton on 20 December 1975 with David Eagles at the controls and test gear in the back seat. This was the first aircraft to be fitted with the twin 27mm IWKA-Mauser cannon in the lower

forward fuselage; this view, however, shows it in its role of 'flying fuel tank' with four 330-gallon (1,500l) drop tanks. Note that the aircraft carries standard RAF red/blue roundels and fin flashes, plus the tri-national roundel on the fin. (BAe)

24. Prototype P-06 pauses on the end of the runway at RAE Farnborough during the 1976 Air Show. Note the drooped leading-edge slats. (Author)

25. Seconds later P-06 roars into the air with full reheat for its demonstration flight. The trailing-edge flaps are fully deployed. (BAe)

▲26

26. The third German-assembled prototype, P-07 (98+06), took to the air on 30 March 1976, with Nils Meister at the controls and Fritz Eckert in the second seat. It was the second avionics test aircraft and assisted P-04 in expanding the terrain-following, ground-mapping, navigation and communications envelopes of the Tornado. (Panavia)

27. The fourth and last British-assembled prototype, P-08 (XX949), flew from Warton on 15 July 1976. The second dual-control aircraft, it was flown by Paul Millett in the front seat, with Ray Woolett in the rear. It assisted P-03 in evaluation of the trainer role, and went on to test avionics and weapons release until 12 June 1979, when the aircraft was lost in a flying accident over the Irish Sea. (BAe)

▼27

28 ▲

28. The second Caselle-assembled prototype, P-09 (X-587), first flew on 5 February 1977 with Pietro Trevisan in command and Manlio Quarantelli in the second seat. This photograph shows the aircraft with drop tanks underwing and ECM pods on the outer pylons. P-09 was the last of the prototypes to fly. (AIT)

29. Later in the test programme, P-09 donned camouflage and concentrated on weapons carriage and release. This photograph shows it carrying a full load: four BL.755 cluster bombs under the fuselage, underwing drop tanks on the inner pylons with AIM-9 Sidewinder AAMs on the inner pylon stub wings; and Sky Shadow ECM pods on the outer pylons, modified to carry recording cameras to film weapons releases. (Panavia)

29 ▼

▲ 30

◄32

30. With airframe No. 10 allocated to static testing, the first of the pre-series aircraft to fly was P-11/98+01. Its first flight took place on the same day as P-09's, 5 February 1977, but from Manching. A dual-control aircraft, it was commanded by Hans-Friedrich Rammensee, with Kurt Schrieber in the rear seat. Inner wing and underfuselage weapons pylons were carried for this flight. (Panavia)

31. The first British pre-series aircraft, P-12 (XZ630), flew from Warton on 14 March 1977 with Tim Ferguson and Roy Kenward on board. This view shows the aircraft on weapons trials, with eight 1,000lb bombs on twin carriers under the fuselage. Like all Tornados now into the programme, the aircraft carries service camouflage. (BAe)

32. The second German pre-series aircraft, P-13 (98+02), in *Luftwaffe* camouflage, flew from Manching on 10 January 1978 with Fritz Soos and Rainer Henke as test crew. This aircraft was the first to feature the slightly 'kinked' tailerons, and the photograph also shows the MW-1 submunition dispenser under the fuselage, a camera pod under the port wing and a Philips BOZ chaff/flare dispenser under the starboard wing. (MBB)

▲ 33

33. The last Italian prototype/pre-series aircraft was
P-14 (X-588), which flew on 8 January 1979 from
Caselle, with Manlio Quarantelli in command and
Egidio Nappi in the second seat. After flight testing it
was used by the Italian Air Force for initial evaluation
work. (AIT)

34. The final British pre-series aircraft, P-15
(XZ631), flew from Warton on 24 November 1978.
This Tornado, flown by Jerry Lee and Jim Evans,
featured a production rear fuselage and 'wet' fin. The
photograph here was taken in September 1982 during
weapons carriage trials at the Aeroplane and
Armament Experimental Establishment at Boscombe
Down; the aircraft has twelve 1,000lb bombs and two
camera pods for recording purposes. (Colin Tarrant,
A&AEE)

35. To Germany went the honour of beginning and
also ending the development of pre-production
Tornados. The last aircraft, P-16 (98+03), flew from
Manching on 29 March 1979 with Armin Krauthan
and Fritz Eckert on board. This photograph shows
drop tanks on the inner wing pylons and 'space
models' of the Sky Shadow ECM pod on the outer
pylons. The aircraft is painted in *Marineflieger*
colours. (MBB)

▲36 ▼37

36. Final assembly of Tornados in Italy is carried out at Caselle, near Turin. This view of the line shows eight aircraft in various stages of completion. (AIT)

37. Within the Panavia consortium, Aeritalia (AIT) is responsible for the construction of all Tornado wings. One complete wing is shown here on its assembly jig. (AIT)

38. The second British-built Tornado prototype, P-03, during weapons carriage trials with four Kormoran anti-ship missiles and Sky Shadow ECM pods. (BAe)

39. Representative of the Italian-assembled prototypes is their first aircraft, P-05 (X-586), seen here taking off from Caselle. The aircraft is camouflaged, and the afterburners are in full reheat. (AIT)

▲40

40. Representative of the RAF Germany units is this Tornado GR.1 of No. XV Squadron. This photograph shows the aircraft framed within its hardened aircraft shelter at RAF Laarbruch and carrying two JP.233 stores under the fuselage. (Barry Ellson, RAFG-PR)

41. No. 16 Squadron, an ex-Buccaneer unit, was the second RAF Germany Tornado unit to form, in February 1984; it is based at Laarbuch, alongside No. XV and the Jaguar GR.1s of No. 2 (or II) Squadron. The Jaguars will eventually give way to a reconnaissance version of the Tornado. (Barry Ellson, RAFG-PR)

42. This view of the flight line at RAF Cottesmore shows a mix of RAF and *Luftwaffe* Tornado IDS aircraft. Each nation at the TTTE retains its identity, although crews and roles may be 'mixed and matched'. (Rolls-Royce)

43. The winter snows of Germany highlight the old style of *Luftwaffe* camouflage for a Tornado IDS of the *WaKo*, which later became *JaboG 38*. (Panavia)

▼41

▲ 44

44. The new style of *Luftwaffe* camouflage is shown to perfection in this view of a *JaboG 32* Tornado. (MTU)

45. A line-up of *Marineflieger* Tornados from *MFG-1* at their base of Jagel near Schleswig. Note that these aircraft are fitted for air-to-air refuelling. (MTU)

46. The Tornado's centre fuselage, including the air intake trunks,

the wing centre-section box and the pivot mechanism, is built by Messerschmitt-Bölkow-Blohm (MBB) in Germany. This photograph shows the final assembly hangar at MBB's Manching facility, with GT-010, a dual-control model for the *Luftwaffe*, almost complete. (MBB)

▼ 45

46 ▶

◄47

48▲

47. As with the airframe, the engines are built by a tri-national consortium, Turbo-Union, which comprises Rolls-Royce (UK), MTU (Germany) and Fiat (Italy). Here an RB.199-34 turbofan engine is being installed in a TTTE Tornado at RAF Cottesmore. (A. J. Ventris, RAF Cottesmore)

48. By far the biggest assembly hall in the programme is that at the British Aerospace (BAe) Warton plant in Lancashire. BAe is responsible for the forward and rear fuselage, including the fin and tailerons. Three lines of Tornados can be seen, with aircraft in various stages of completion. (BAe)

49. The pilot's 'office' of a Tornado IDS is dominated by the Marconi head-up display, the dark circle below it being the Ferranti moving-map display. The flight instruments are largely

conventional, although ergonomically laid out, and the cockpit does seem somewhat old-fashioned when compared with the VDU-dominated panels in current US aircraft such as the F/A-18 and the 'glass cockpits' of next-generation aircraft. (MBB)

50. The rear cockpit for the weapons system operator (still called a navigator in the RAF) is the heart of the Tornado's weapons and navigation system. This view shows one of the prototypes: the four 'dial' instruments to the left of the moving-map display in the centre should mirror the visual display unit (VDU) on its right. This particular rear cockpit is of a dual-control aircraft (note the throttles and control column), the sidestick to the right being part of the weapons aiming system. (BAe)

49▼

50▼

▲51　　　▼52

51. The first production
Tornado for the RAF, rolled
out at Warton on 5 June 1979,
was a dual-control version
(hence the company
identification number BT-001),
which is designated GR.1(T) in
the RAF. (Author)

52. BT-001's first flight on 10
July 1979 lasted 1 hour 27
minutes. The pilot, David
Eagles, said on landing, 'The
standard is exceptionally high
for a first production aircraft
and this reflects great credit on
everyone concerned'. (BAe)

53. An RAF Tornado GR.1(T)
of the Tri-national Tornado
Training Establishment, seen in
1981, shortly after its formation
in January of that year. The
TTTE is responsible for
training all IDS aircraft
crewmen to a competent
standard before they depart to
their respective national
weapons training units. All staff
and students are mixed; for
example, an Italian aircraft
might fly with a German pilot
and an RAF navigator.
(Author)

54. This fine study of three TTTE Tornados shows a pair of RAF aircraft with a *Luftwaffe* example. The wings are at mid-sweep. (Sgt. Brian Lawrence)

▲55

55. For RAF Tornado GR.1 aircrew, the first stop after TTTE is the Tornado Weapons Conversion Unit (TWCU) at RAF Honington. Here the pilots and navigators learn to 'fight' their aircraft as a team. The TWCU has now been allocated the 'shadow' designation of No. 45 Squadron. The aircraft shown wears the squadron markings on the nose and the TWCU badge on the fin. Note the chin fairing under the nose, which houses the Ferranti laser ranger and marked-target seeker. (RAF Honington)

56. The first RAF unit to form on the Tornado GR.1 was No. 9 Squadron based alongside the TWCU at Honington, in June 1982. This photograph was taken on 14 March 1984. The aircraft carries

two 1,000lb bombs under the fuselage, two drop tanks and a pair of Marconi Sky Shadow ECM pods. (Author)

57. This 1983 photograph shows a pair of Tornado GR.1s of No. 9 Squadron laying retarded 1,000lb bombs over the ranges at West Freugh in Scotland. Note the retarding parachute on the bomb nearest the water. (BAe)

58. Although following No. 9 Squadron in numerical order, No. 27 was the third RAF unit to equip with the Tornado GR.1, in August 1983. Based at RAF Marham, a team from this squadron swept the board at the Strategic Air Command bombing competition in 1985 (repeating No. 617's performance the year before). (R. L. Ward)

▼56

57 ▲   58 ▼

▲ 59   ▼ 60

38

59. In 1984, aircraft from both No. 9 and No. 27 Squadrons took part in a flypast over London to mark H.M. The Queen's official birthday. Considering the Tornado's low-level attack role, it is unlikely that this 'diamond nine' formation will be a regular sight in the sky. (Sgt. J. Upsall, MoD PR)

60. The second RAF unit to acquire Tornados was the famed No. 617 Squadron in May 1983; the unit is based at RAF Marham in Norfolk alongside No. 27 (as well as the Victor K.2 tankers of No. 55). The aircraft in this photograph is accompanied by a No. 1 TWU Hawk and shows the undersurface camouflage, a continuation of the uppersurface pattern in a 'wraparound' scheme. A Sky Shadow ECM pod and a PEAB BOZ chaff/flare dispenser are

fitted. (John Green, MoD Rep-S)

61. On the ground, all Tornado squadrons are housed in a collection of hardened aircraft shelters; here a No. 617 Squadron aircraft is being pushed back into its HAS at Marham. In 1984 an RAF team from No. 617 competed in the Strategic Air Command annual bombing competition – the first time an RAF Tornado unit had taken part – and won two of the three trophies for which it was eligible to compete. (MoD Rep-S)

62. RAF Germany is to deploy the bulk of RAF Tornado GR.1 squadrons. Based at Bruggen, No. 14 Squadron is relatively new on the scene, forming in October 1985. This is one of its aircraft. (RAF Bruggen)

62 ▼

▲63   ▼64

63. The first RAF Germany unit to form was No. 15 Squadron (or, as the aircrew prefer, No. XV Squadron) which exchanged its Buccaneer S.2s for Tornados in October 1983. The unit is based at Laarbuch, near the Dutch border. (Barry Ellson, RAFG-PR)
64. With an example of the unit's previous mount, the Jaguar GR.1, in the lead, a Tornado GR.1 of No. 17 Squadron flies over the snow-swept landscape of central Germany. Based at Bruggen, No. 17 was formed in March 1985. (BAe)
65. The conversion of No. 20 Squadron in June 1984 to the

Tornado GR.1 also saw the unit move from Bruggen (where it had existed as a Jaguar unit) to Laarbruch. (No. 20 Sqn. via R. L. Ward)
66. RAFG Tornado GR.1s from No. 31 Squadron. Based at Bruggen, this unit formed in November 1984, having previously been equipped with Jaguars. Note that only two of the aircraft (furthest away from the camera) are carrying the chin fairing for the LRMTS. (BAe)

▲ 67

67. Air-to-air refuelling is an important aspect of Tornado operations. It was used early in the test programme to expand the flight times of aircraft in the air, and operationally it will increase the range, or the loiter time on combat air patrol (CAP), of the aircraft. Here the first Air Defence Variant, A-01, and the pre-series IDS P-15 are about to make contact with a No. 57 Squadron Victor K.2 tanker. The IDS (GR.1) aircraft have an externally plumbed refuelling probe mounted alongside the starboard side of the cockpit, while the ADV has an internally mounted probe which retracts into the port side. (BAe)

68. Of the three nations involved in the Tornado programme, only the RAF has a dedicated tanker fleet. The German Navy and Italian Air Force have, however, acquired 'buddy' packs to enable their Tornados to enjoy the benefits of AAR. It is ironic, therefore, to see two aircraft in RAF markings carrying out AAR 'buddy-buddy'

trials: here P-15 is receiving fuel from P-03 equipped with a Sargent Fletcher 'buddy' pack. (BAe)

69. One of the new weapons systems developed for use by RAF Tornados is the Hunting Engineering JP.233 airfield attack system. Here two JP.233 containers are seen mounted below a Tornado GR.1. (BAe)

70. This view clearly shows the deployment of the two types of sub-munitions dispensed by the JP.233 system. The smaller sub-munitions dropping from the front part of the container are HB.875 area-denial mines, left to dampen the enthusiasm of airfield repair parties tasked with rectifying the damage left by the SG.357 parachute-retarded runway-cratering munitions dropped from the rear part of the store. Some 215 HB.875s are contained in each dispenser, with 30 SG.357s. (Hunting)

▼ 68

69 ▲   70 ▼

▲ 71

71. To replace the Jaguar GR.1 reconnaissance aircraft, the Tornado is to take on another small modification, without detracting from its ability to perform strike missions. The guns are removed and replaced by a sideways-looking infra-red system and an IR Linescan 4000 surveillance system. (BAe)

72. Another new weapon for RAF Tornados is the BAe ALARM (Air-Launched Anti-Radiation Missile), used to knock out enemy AAA radars. This photograph shows the weapon in close-up – the first captive-carry trials missiles, which were successfully

demonstrated in February 1986. Note the triple carriage configuration on the inner wing pylons. (BAe)

73. Seven ALARMS are seen on this Tornado although in practice fewer would be carried and other weapons, such as the BL.755 cluster bomb, would be used to take out the remnants of the AAA sites. (BAe)

74. This unusual photograph of an Italian Tornado shows an aircraft of *6° Stormo* flying over the sea with water vapour condensing above the wings. (Panavia)

▼ 72

▲75　▼76

75. The third prototype Tornado ADV, alias the F.2, photographed during weapons trials. Note the condensation coming from the wing tips. (BAe)

76. Looking like an example of the latest form of computer-generated imagery for simulation systems is this low-level view of a Tornado F.2 of No. 229 OCU, RAF Coningsby. (BAe)

77. This fine study of the first production Tornado F.3 with Mk.104 RB.199 engines and lengthened tailpipes emphasizes the smooth lines of this variant of what once was disparagingly called 'Mother Riley's Cardboard Aeroplane'. (BAe)

▲ 78

78. In May 1983 three Tornado GR.1s from the Tornado Weapons Conversion Unit joined the *Red Arrows* for a visit to the United States. This formation photograph shows the three Tornados leading the Hawk T.1s over the coast of East Anglia prior to departure. (BAe)

79. Although Oman was the first export customer to order the Tornado (in its ADV/F.3 form) in August 1985, it is Saudi Arabia which will receive the first export aircraft. The first dozen of her order for 48 Tornado IDS have been diverted from the RAF's GR.1 line, and deliveries began in April/May 1986. This photograph shows the desert camouflage adopted for the Royal Saudi Air Force, for which 24 Tornado F.3s have also been ordered. (BAe)

80. Resplendent in the MoD(PE) colour scheme known to many as 'raspberry ripple' is Tornado GR.1(T) ZA326, which joined the test

▼ 79

fleet at RAE Bedford in July 1983. The aircraft was from the first production batch for the RAF, but was badly damaged by fire during ground runs; broken down into its national elements, it was repaired and reassembled at Warton late in 1982. Its acquisition by the RAE will ensure that the Establishment has one example from the current generation of aircraft with which to carry out its variety of trials and experiments. (Peter Hudson, RAE Bedford)

81. First of a kind: on 6 May 1985 Sqn. Ldr. Rod Sargeant of No. 16 Squadron at Laarbruch became the first pilot in the world to log 1,000 flying hours in the Tornado. This photograph shows Sqn. Ldr. Sargeant being presented with an appropriate Panavia badge by Laarbruch's Station Commander, Gp. Capt. David Cousins. (Cpl. Dave Murray, RAFG-PR)

80▲   81▼

▲82 ▼83

84 ▲

82. One day after BAe rolled out its first production Tornado GR.1, MBB did the same for the *Luftwaffe* on 6 June 1979 at the Manching Flight Test Centre. (Panavia)

83. GT-001, the first production Tornado IDS for the *Luftwaffe*, made its maiden flight on 27 July 1979. Coded 43+01, the aircraft is seen here overflying Manching. (MBB)

84. Seen on the day the Tri-national Tornado Training Establishment (TTTE) was commissioned, 29 January 1981, is this *Luftwaffe* IDS in its original green/grey/black camouflage scheme.

Note the TTTE emblem on the fin and the identity 'buzz' number. (Author)

85. Weapons training for both the *Luftwaffe* and the *Marineflieger* is carried out by one unit. Originally known as the *Waffenausbildungskomponente* (*WaKo*) when it formed at Erding in February 1982, it later became *JaboG 38* when it moved to Jever in August 1983. This photograph shows two *WaKo* Tornados in 1982. (Panavia)

85 ▼

▲ 86   ▼ 87

88 ▲

86. *JaboG 31* was the first operational squadron to be equipped with Tornado in the *Luftwaffe*, forming at Norvenich in August 1983. This aircraft is in the new camouflage scheme of dark grey, dark green and medium green overall. The rather obvious stencilling and walk markings would be overpainted in the event of hostilities. (MBB)

87. The next *Luftwaffe* unit (in numerical order) is *JaboG 32*. which formed at Lechfeld in August 1984. This photograph shows four Tornados in the squadron's maintenance hangar, painted in the new colour scheme. (MTU)

88. Two Tornados of *JaboG 38* (formerly *WaKo*) show the two camouflage schemes. The old scheme is carried by the aircraft nearest the camera. (MBB)

89. A 'twinstick' Tornado of *JaboG 33*, which formed at Buchel in August 1985. The aircraft is on loan to *JaboG 32* prior to issue to *JaboG 33* and was photographed at RAF Cottesmore on the occasion of the fifth anniversary of the TTTE in July 1985. (D. Mason)

89 ▼

▲ 90

90. This *WaKo* aircraft, seen at the Hanover Air Show in May 1982, is equipped with the Mehrzweck-Waffensystem-1 (MW-1) under the belly, inner wing tanks with AIM-9s on stub pylons and a BOZ chaff/flare pod on the outer starboard pylon. (Author)

91. This photograph shows the distribution of submunitions from the MW-1 dispenser during trials. The MW-1 system, for use against armour and enemy air bases, has been developed by MBB, with RTG/Diehl responsible for the KB.44 submunitions. (MBB)

92. The latest version of the Tornado under development is an Electronic Combat/Reconnaissance (ECR) aircraft, allocations in the German FY86 R&D budget marking the launch of a programme for 35 such machines. The order was placed on 11 June 1986. As well as provision for the AGM-88A HARM anti-radar missile, the ECR will feature FLIR and IRLS systems and other avionic improvements. This photograph is of an artist's impression. (MBB)

93. The German Navy and Italian Air Force have opted for a multi-sensor reconnaissance pod rather than the integral recce suite of the RAF's GR.1s. This photograph shows the pod under the belly of P-01. (MBB)

▼ 91

▲ 94

94. The first operational wing of German Tornados was *Marinefleigergeschwader 1* (*MFG-1*), which formed at Jagel in Schleswig in July 1982. This photograph shows a formation of four *MFG-1* aircraft in 'clean' configuration and resplendent in the standard dark sea grey/white colour scheme. (Panavia)

95. An *MFG-1* Tornado touching down at its base at Jagel. The main role of the squadron is anti-shipping strike, and the aircraft will be armed with the MBB Kormoran ASM. (MTU)

96. Trials began in December 1985 for the carriage and use of the Texas Instruments AGM-88A HARM (High-speed Anti-Radar Missile) on a *Marineflieger* Tornado. This photograph shows an air-carriage trial of a four-missile configuration. (MBB)

97. In 1985, the *Marineflieger* began to evaluate a new three-tone grey camouflage scheme for its aircraft, as carried here by an *MFG-1* Tornado. The in-flight refuelling probe installation on the starboard side of the fuselage, below the cockpit line, can be seen. (MBB)

98. (Next spread) Seven Italian Tornados on the flight line at Caselle in Northern Italy await delivery to the *Aeronautica Militare Italiana*. The disposition of the 99 production Tornados plus the refurbished P-14 pre-series aircraft is as follows: eighteen aircraft each to the *154°*, *156°* and *51° Gruppo* (Squadron); ten aircraft to the TTTE in the UK; and 36 aircraft to reserve to maintain unit strengths during overhaul and maintenance and as attrition aircraft. (AIT)

▼ 95

96 ▲   97 ▼

▲ 99

100 ▲

◀101

99. Masquerading as I-40 of the TTTE for the commissioning ceremony at RAF Cottesmore on 29 January 1981 is P-14; the markings were added specifically for this occasion. (R. L. Ward)

100. The real I-40, seen at TTTE in November 1982. Note the change in style of the lettering for the 'buzz' number and also the staining on the lower forward fin as a result of use of the reverse thrust 'buckets' on the RB.199 engines. (R. L. Ward)

101. An IDS of *154° Gruppo* of the *6° Stormo* (Wing) of the *AMI* seen on take-off in 'clean' configuration. Note the afterburner cones, and the main undercarriage almost retracted. (AIT)

103▲

◀104

102. Another *154° Gruppo* aircraft, seen at RAF Cottesmore on 15 July 1985. The fin markings are slightly different from those seen in the previous photograph. The *154° Gruppo/6° Stormo* is based at Ghedi. (D. Mason)

103. Seen at the same time as the previous aircraft is this *156° Gruppo/36° Stormo* aircraft with four drop tanks, two under the wings and two under the fuselage. The *Gruppo* is based at Gioia del Colle, and one flight is equipped with the Kormoran ASM for the maritime attack role. (D. Mason)

104. An artist's impression of the RAF's air defence variant, the Tornado F.2, launching the Sky Flash AAM. (Image in Industry/BAe)

PANAVIA TORNADO
ROLL OUT OF 1ST
F. Mk.2 PROTOTYPE
9TH AUGUST 1979

▲ 106

105. (Previous spread) The first Tornado F.2 ADV aircraft, in a white/grey/black colour scheme, seen at the roll-out on 9 August 1979. In addition to dummy Sky Flash AAMs under the fuselage, the aircraft is equipped with two dummy AIM-9 Sidewinders on the inner pylon stub wings and long-range drop tanks on the main inner pylons. (Author)

106. The first of three pre-series ADV aircraft is seen almost complete in this May 1979 photograph. The aircraft is in the yellow ochre primer finish and is fitted with dummy Sky Flash missiles. (BAe)

107. The first photograph released, in August 1979, of the Marconi (now GEC) Avionics AI.24 air interception radar, sometimes called Foxhunter, which is the 'eyes' of the Tornado F.2. The cassegrain antenna of this pulse-doppler radar is clearly visible. (GEC Avionics)

▼ 107

108▲

108. This close-up view of the inner pylon clearly shows the stub-wing mounting for the AIM-9 Sidewinder and the 330-gallon (1,500l) external long-range tank. Note also the landing light on the inside of the main undercarriage door. (Author)
109. The Tornado F.2 first flew on 27 October 1979 with David Eagles at the controls and Roy Kenward in the navigator's seat.

This view shows the aircraft with wings fully swept back, while black dummy Sky Flash AAMs are clearly seen in their staggered positions. The lengthened nose and fuselage, together with the inner fixed wing leading edge 'nibs', make for a more aesthetically appealing aircraft. (BAe)

109▼

110. Another photograph of the first F.2 in flight shows the full complement of 'missiles' and tanks. Early in 1982, this aircraft, in this configuration, flew 325nm (602km) from Warton out to the North Sea at high altitude, descended to medium level for a combat air patrol lasting 2 hours 20 minutes, returned to base at high level, loitered at low altitude for 15 minutes and landed with five per cent reserves of internal fuel after a total sortie lasting 4 hours 13 minutes. (Panavia/BAe)

111. The second F.2, A-02, here seen during its first flight on 18 July 1980, was the only dual-control prototype. Flown on this occasion by Paul Millett and Roy Kenward, its main task was weapons system integration and development. (BAe)

112. Later in the development programme, A-02 was fitted with RB.199 Mk.104 engines with a 14in (36cm) extension to the reheat pipes, an additional burning volume which gives the aircraft 12–15 per cent more thrust than the Mk.103-equipped Tornado. A-02 also featured a digital engine control unit, developed by Lucas Aerospace. (BAe)

▲110

111▲ 112▼

▲113

113. A-03 in a colour scheme more representative of the RAF's air defence force. The aircraft's first flight was on 18 November 1980, with Peter Gordon-Johnson and Leslie Hurst as crew. Representative of a production F.2, this Tornado ADV was destined to undertake radar development trials with the AI.24 system. Note the trials camera mounted on the forward radar warning receiver fairing at the leading edge of the fin. (HQ Strike Command)

114. The first two production Tornado F.2 aircraft were unveiled at Warton on 28 March 1984. Pictured nearest the camera is the nose of ZD900 with its in-flight refuelling probe deployed; further

from the camera is ZD899 on jacks in a representative flying attitude. (R. L. Ward)

115. Another view of ZD899 reveals the enhanced lines of the forward fuselage. The aircraft carries its full complement of missiles (Sky Flash and Sidewinder), plus long-range tanks. (R. L. Ward)

116. The first RAF unit to receive the Tornado F.2 was No. 229 Operational Conversion Unit. BAe Warton delivered the first two machines on 5 November 1984, both aircraft having duel controls. This photograph shows 'AA' (ZD901) landing at RAF Coningsby, home of No. 229 OCU. (BAe)

▼114

115▲ 116▼

▲117

117. Two Tornado F.2s from No. 229 OCU, RAF Coningsby. (BAe)

118. Following the development trials of A-02 with the RB.199 Mk.104 engines, it was decided to install these from the 19th aircraft onwards. In addition, the aircraft would feature automatic wing sweep, a dual inertial navigation system and provision for the Joint Tactical Information Distribution System, making for a change in designation to Tornado F.3 by the RAF. This photograph shows the first production F.3 on its first flight from Warton on 20 November 1985. (BAe)

▼118